D1412334

More Than Friends

More Than Friends

Poems from Him and Her

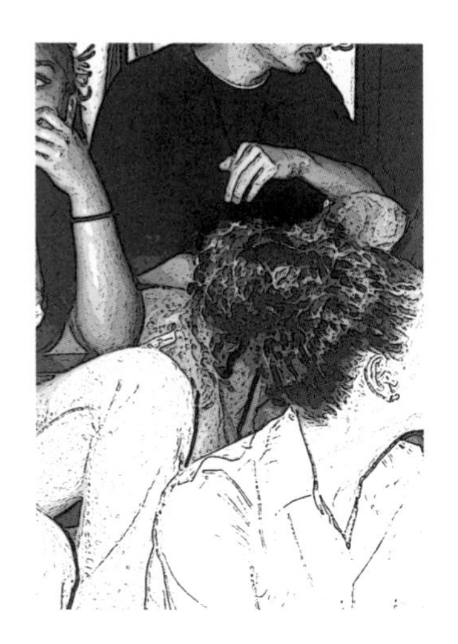

Sara Holbrook and
Allan Wolf

WORDSONG
HONESDALE, PENNSYLVANIA

To Stephanie, with love

—*S.H.*

For Mario and Possum—more than brothers

—*A.W.*

Thanks to the following readers who commented on early versions of the manuscript: teachers Lee Corey, Lee Ann Spillane, Julie Powell, and Pat Kraus and all of their students; Bob Falls; Emily-Grace Sarver Wolf; and Maxwell and Franklin Salinger.

Jacket photograph by Steven B. Smith
Photographs on pages 31 and 39 by Edie Moon.
All others by Sara Holbrook and Allan Wolf.
Graphic artwork by Sara Holbrook

"A Secret Sonnet" first appeared in *Walking on the Boundaries of Change* by Sara Holbrook, Wordsong, 1998.

Wordsong
An Imprint of Boyds Mills Press, Inc.
815 Church Street, Honesdale, Pennsylvania 18431
Printed in China

Library of Congress Cataloging-in-Publication Data

Holbrook, Sara.
More than friends : poems from him and her / Sara Holbrook and Allan Wolf. — 1st ed.
p. cm.
ISBN 978-1-59078-587-4 (alk. paper)
1. Interpersonal relations in adolescence—Juvenile poetry.
2. Young adult poetry, American. I. Wolf, Allan. II. Title.
PS3558.O347745M67 2008
811'.54—dc22
2007050282

First edition
Designed by Tim Gillner
The text of this book is set in 10-point Sabon.

10 9 8 7 6 5 4 3 2 1

The two sexes mutually corrupt and improve each other.

—Mary Wollstonecraft

Contents

More Than Friends

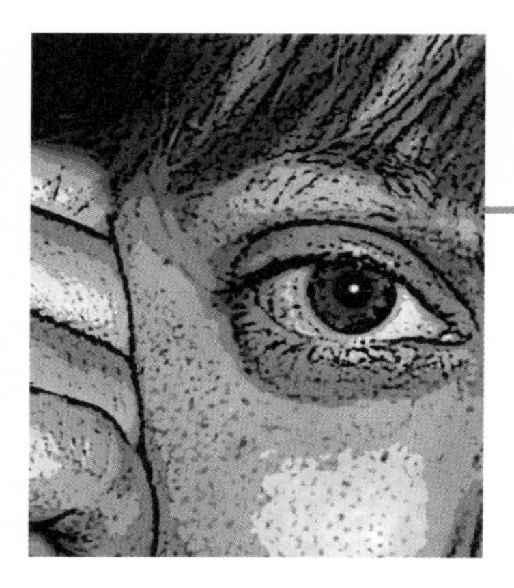

What Do You Do When She Looks at You?

Become unglued
and crimson-hued?
Turn away,
afraid to stare?
Bury your face in your biology book?

Or return the look?

What do you do when she looks at you?
Shout her name
from atop your chair?
Flare your nostrils?
Pose and flex?
Bellow like a buffalo bull in love?
Yodel like a loin-cloth-clad Tarzan?

Or take her hand?

What do you do when she looks at you?
A hundred things I could have done.
A hundred words lay on my tongue.
A hundred pickup lines marched by—

I just said, "Hi."

What Do You Do When He Looks at You?

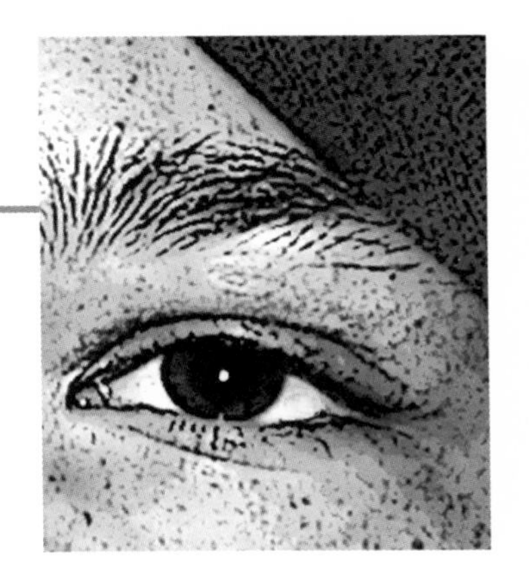

For sure, if he is looking here's the rule:
Stand tall, inhale and tummy-hold, then try
to sneak a peek but still maintain your cool.
Be subtle, private, ask your friends to spy.
Adjust your belt, fluff hair, and moisten teeth,
then stall, turn back, search purse, and check your phone.
Don't panic or betray your knees are weak.
Don't mope or look pathetic when alone.
Don't burp or scratch your nose or pick or pull.
Don't be a tramp, but you should show some skin.
Don't wolf down food, pretend that you are full.
And look so int'rested, just not in him.
These rules are set in concrete. Don't ask why.
You have to follow them, OR . . . just say, "Hi."

She Says All Boys Are Thoughtless Jerks

She says all boys are thoughtless jerks
(except, of course, for me).
She says I'm not "like all the other guys."
All boys are fraught with flaws and quirks
(except, of course, for me).
Because I'm not "like all the other guys."

And yet she keeps on dating jerks
and then complains to me.
She turns on gushing waterworks
and says, "How can it be
that every boy's a thoughtless jerk?"
(except, of course, for me).
She says I'm not "like all the other guys."

Each time she says I'm special
(not "like all the other guys"),
I'm growing more invisible
before her very eyes.
And next time, when she finds me gone,
she'll say, "I'm not surprised"
and tell her friends I turned out just
"like all the other guys."

Free verse with refrain

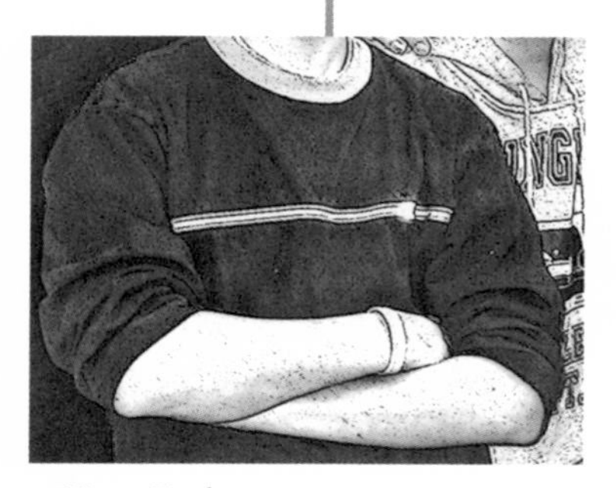

Her

Boys are thoughtless jerks.
Show-offs, player wannabees.
It's all about them.
Teasing means that they like you?
Fact: Boys only want one thing.

He Says All Girls Are Bubbleheads

Him
Girls are bubbleheads.
Skirts. Hair. Hips. Lips. Mystery.
Giggle. Gossip. Cry.
Travel in packs. Straight-A smart.
Watch guys play. And never fart.

Tanka

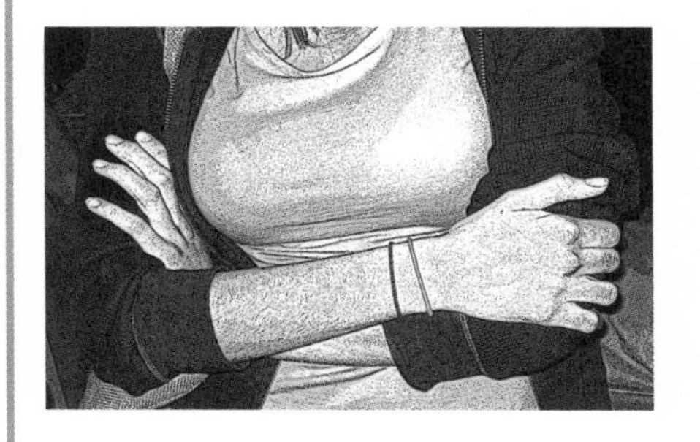

Those other girls aren't me.
I'm not your property. I don't
like second place. I won't
pretend I'm dumb, and don't presume
I'm thinking bride and groom
or that I'm so consumed by love,
a mere reflection of
you. I am not above the rest,
but if you pass the test
you might sample the best right here.
You'll never have to fear
that I will drop a tear on you.
Like I'd give one boo-hoo
to manipulate. True, I can
without lifting a hand
washrag-twist out a man, but I
would never bat an eye
to cover up a lie (blink, blink)
or drive you to the brink.
Oh, I confess, I think you're fine
(I checked you from behind).
If you'll respect my mind, you'll see
I'm not like them. I'm me.

Luc bat

Veggie Panini Is the Answer to Everything

I don't know what makes
two people "just friends" on Thursday
and "more than friends" on Friday.
But today was Friday.
The one-hundredth look
was different from the first ninety-nine.
Today's "Hi" was different
from every "Hi" that came before.

I swear I wasn't smitten,
but then . . . the lunch bell rang.
And there you are:
    sitting at our usual lunchroom table
    (has she always sat like that?)
    and we look at each other
    (has she always looked like that?)
    and we say "Hi"—
    (has she always talked like that?)
    eating what looks like
    (has she always chewed like that?)
    just a sandwich but what you inform me
    is actually "a veggie panini."

"A veggie *what*?" I ask and smile
as wide as a door on well-oiled hinges.
And you smile back the same and answer,
"Paah-NEE-nee. Paah-NEE-nee. A veggie panini."
In English class I even look it up.

"Paah-NEE-nee. Paah-NEE-nee. A veggie panini."
I whisper it into the electric air and picture
your lips, your smile, your look, your lunch, your hair.
I mutter it all the way home:
"Veggie panini. Veggie panini."
I hug my mom (first time in like a year).
"And how was your day?" my mother asks.
"Veggie paah-NEE-nee" is my answer.

Veggie panini is the answer to everything.

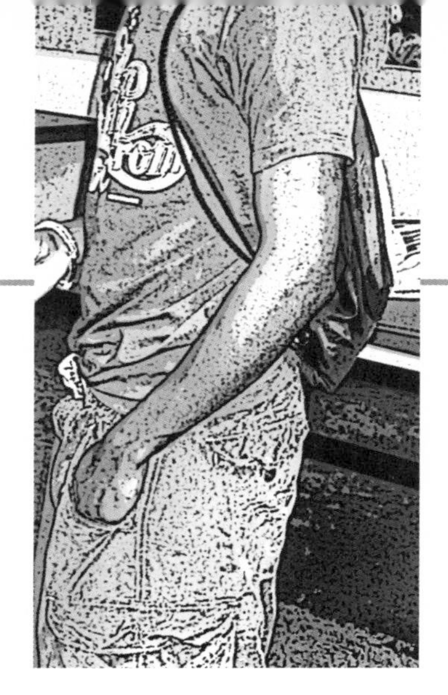

He's Not a Fake

He's not a fake,
        all flirty.
Told no jokes down and dirty,
        just watchful.
No roller-coaster rides,
        no fireworks,
no fast breaks,
        or clean jerks,
                just watchful.
Silently steady,
        narrow-eyed, ready.
Not just in a word,
        he was in a state—
                he was watchful.

Shopping

Her
Destination: Mall.
Wandering is half the fun.
Does this lipstick match?
Look and dream, you never know.
Would he love me in these jeans?

Him
Guys don't go shopping.
Pants, shirts, shoes, socks, boxers, belts:
they all just appear.
Eggs, bread, milk, ice cream—appear.
It's magic. Guys do *not* shop.

Hair

Him
Short is less trouble.
Bleaching looks cool, but it hurts.
Dab of gel's okay.
Big perm? No. Spiky grunge? Yes.
Easy low-tech dos win out.

Her
Fluffed, braided, or waved.
Try to frame the face just right.
Soft and touchable.
But if it's pure perfection,
mess with it and you're dead.

Underwear

Her
Straps, strings, little things
mostly hidden undercover.
Black, pink, leopard print,
lacy, or sturdy cotton—
choices made to match my mood.

Him
Underwear in brief:
mostly equipped with front flaps;
tightie whites, jockstraps,
low-rise, boxer, bikini,
jumbo, or teeny-weeny.

I Hope She Likes the Way I Wear My Tee

I hope she likes the way I wear my tee—
my sleeves rolled up, my shirttail hanging loose.
'Course I don't dress for her; I dress for me.
If how I look's not me, then what's the use?
I hope she likes the way my blue jeans sag—
the boxer shorts exposed. The belt bum-wrapped.
I wear 'em inside out to show the tag:
DKNY—Hilfiger—Nike—Gap.
But being fashion-forward isn't free,
especially when styles change every day.
My look is wrong if how I look ain't me.
I'll be myself. I'm better off that way.
I'll just be cool when I see her today.
It's time! You think my outfit looks okay?

You Think I Dressed Myself for Him Today?

You think I dressed myself for him today?
The herbal scent? The gloss? It's just for me.
How could you think? As if. Way wrong. No way.
Last night I read some dull, dry history,
I cruised the Net (briefly) for makeup tips,
I ate, cleaned up, got sooo bored by TV.
Big deal. A makeover from toes to lips
was just time-fill, a thing I did for me.
And just because I shaved, tweezed, plucked and trimmed,
and whitened teeth, it's not like I'm obsessed.
These jeans? This low-slung rhinestone belt? For him?
The seven times I practiced getting dressed?
You think I'd do all this for someone else?
Untrue. I found my best side for myself.

Mother

Him
Mother is the one
clutching my frayed sweater's thread,
I grow away from her
into the brisk winter world
unraveling into a man.

Her
Mothers embarrass.
Mine thinks she knows *the* right way
like she holds a map.
Her past is not my future.
I will never be like her.

Father

Her

I watch Dad dozing,
pretending to watch the game.
Even when he's home
he drifts just beyond my reach.
Notice me! I need a hug.

Him

Father is the nest,
yet tall and strong as the tree
shading the hot son,
teaching the fledgling to fly,
losing leaves to ease the fall.

I Can Only Hold My Breath

I can only hold my breath
When *he* comes to meet Mom and Dad.
I'm about to choke to death.

I know if this meeting goes bad
We'll never go out again.
It would be a total disaster, more sad

Than words could ever express.
When the last guy licked his knife
At dinner, a move that failed to impress

My mom, who (I could tell) considered him lowlife,
And when he blurted out he liked the Mets—
My dad cut a look at his wife,

Which is about as bad as it can get.
After that, they teamed up together
And there was no beating that mind-set.

I want this to go better,
And I want him to like them, too.
But as he sits there, hands folded, looking redder

And REDDER, I wonder how he could like this zoo
I call a family. My brother sits with his finger up his nose
At dinner. Mom hums. Dad belches. I can barely chew.

I hate my mother's frumpy clothes.
And my dad's jokes are far from the best.
Does he think I'll grow up like these zeros?

I'd rather be hung by my thumbs or put to death
By a dull chain saw or an army of killer bees.
What can I possibly do? I hold my breath.

Meeting Your Mom and Dad

Cool and thick the plastic sticks
to the sweat on my thighs.
I fidget on your parents' couch,
its waxy protection clinging
to its cushions and folds.

Sure and quick, their darting fish
flash under my eyes.
I look at what I mustn't touch:
Angel rocking water under fanning paroxysm;
Angel blowing kisses to my finger through the glass.

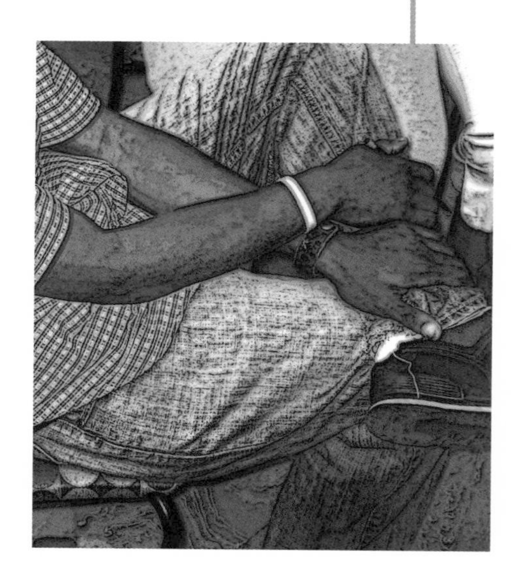

This is the way it's done, I think,
this painful thing I have to do.
This portal to another world.
This trial by fire. This ritual.
To dare to fly into the Sun.
To break bread with the guardians of the gate.

By 8 p.m. the dinner is all gone.

Porch light lit, I touch your lips.
We flounder for good-byes.
I hear plastic sag under your father's slouch,
the fish tank murmur,
and your mother's muffled voice.

So I hurry away
on your gift of Icarus wings,
your mother's lasagna in my stomach,
the smell of you on my clothes,
your phone number
in my pocket.

Tests

Her
Focusing on blanks,
A, B, C, all of above.
Your eyes lock on mine.
Brain now a washing machine—
facts, letters tumble and spin.

Him
Tests are less trouble
for me since I have met you.
Is it possible?
Can having you in my life
increase the size of my brain?

Foolish

Her
Words that won't come out.
Stargazing on railroad tracks.
Snubbing Cynthia.
Wearing flip-flops in the snow.
Talking heads who just can't know.

Him
My fly was open.
Spilled our popcorn on the floor.
Stepped on your foot—twice.
Yet the more the night went wrong,
The more you and I felt right.

Making the First Move

Shoulders touching, we sit
in the dark and listen to the movie drone.
Eyes front, I face the screen
and pretend to watch and care.
Pretend my veins aren't filled with sand.
I will the sweat to return to my pores,
but my locker-room confidence is gone
like bats from the rafters of a twilight barn.

I estimate the distance to her knee
at about . . . three football fields.
And suddenly I'm thinking
of my football moves.
My soccer moves.
My hands moving on a chessboard.
My feet moving on a skateboard.
My family moving out of state.
Moving to another universe. To the Outer Rim,
to the dead planet Dagobah where Yoda hides.
What would Yoda do? I ask.
Use the Force I would, the master replies.

So I close my eyes and mentally
shift all resources to my comatose hand.
The life-force begins to drain from me
yet my massive arm moves—
a quick robotic lurch—into the air.
With all the grace of a John Deere backhoe,
the arm swings up and out and drops,
crash-landing for the touchdown.
Neil Armstrong, successfully landing on the moon,
could not have felt the same fear and awe.

All is quiet.

On its denim-clad landing pad my hand lies still.
Perhaps it is stunned,
perhaps playing possum.
Or perhaps it really is dead, no longer a part of me.
I watch it proudly from the corner of my eye—
my used-to-be-mine hand—
happily paralyzed, beautifully abandoned
on the warm surface of an alien world.

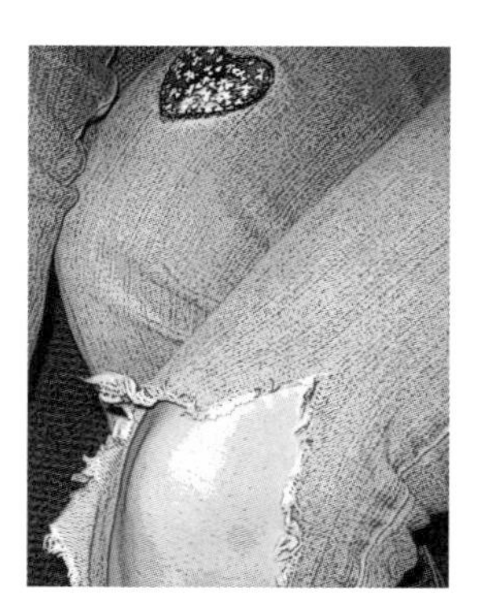

Do Not Bolt Screaming, Clutching All Your Stuff

Do not bolt screaming, clutching all your stuff.
His hand is light and warm against the knee.
Is it too much or is it just enough?

All smart girls know flirtation is a bluff.
First smiles and winks are offered easily.
Do not bolt screaming, clutching all your stuff.

If he is gentle, not a bit too rough,
the brain may overthink obsessively:
is it too much or is it just enough?

The natural progression is a touch.
A girl must choose to lean his way or flee.
Do not bolt screaming, clutching all your stuff.

Ears pound, the heart is stomping, face is flushed.
The drumming draws toward love's mystery.
Is it too much or is it just enough?

This wildfire, started by a finger brush,
can't be contained or fed offhandedly.
Do not bolt screaming, clutching all your stuff.
Is it too much or is it just enough?

Sex

Him
Life breaks in.
Wipes away the little boy
like an ocean wave
reshaping the blissful beach
into a baffled castle.

Her
Cosmo, MTV,
open-mouthed soap opera kisses,
the Swimsuit Issue,
play tug-of-war with parents.
When and where do I fit in?

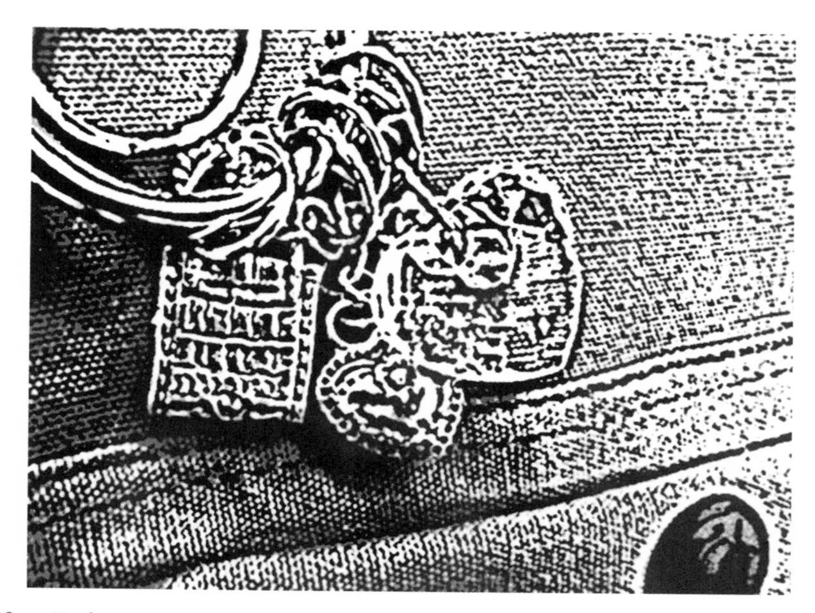

A Secret Sonnet

I gently plucked a kiss from your left ear
and softly slipped it there, beneath your chin.
Sh . . . sh . . . we mustn't let the parents hear.
Shriek! They'll stomp and holler, "Mortal sin!"
Let's not announce this so our friends will know.
Please, keep this interaction off the news.
They'll set alarms, keep asking, "Yes or no?"
Ticktock—the clock—and we will have to choose.
On one side, half will moan we went too far.
The rest will mock us, screaming out for more.
Reactions! You will spring to arm your guard
and I will shrink to barricade the door.
Entrenched in public, we will sadly miss
the private chance to savor—just one kiss.

How Can I Even Hope to Keep This In?

"Love and a cough cannot be hid."
—George Herbert

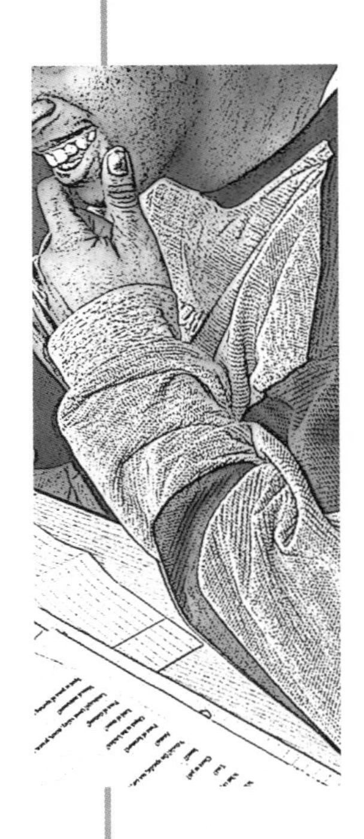

I know the guys will see it on my face.
I cannot help but wear this silly grin.
Some kisses are not difficult to trace.
They'll see you hidden just below my skin.
My friends aren't bright but even *they* will see
the way your presence causes me to blush,
the way I've started writing poetry,
the way I talk a little bit too much.
The kiss you softly slipped beneath my chin;
the kiss I lightly left behind your ear:
how can I even hope to keep this in?
I want to shout for all the world to hear.
So tell my lips to hush and they'll obey;
the rest of me keeps giving us away.

Music

Him

Bass-beat boom of doom.
Wailing-guitar distortion.
Drum-kit thundercrash.
Raging screams assault and slash.
Soothing homework mood music.

Her

Download poetry.
Singing along in private.
Love songs make me cry.
Carrying tunes in my head.
The rhythm's in me. Let's dance.

Relax

Her
Vanilla candle.
Cruising a mind-skate daydream.
Nothing overdue.
I call you up on the phone.
Should I take a bubble bath?

Him
Out of bed by one.
Big game on television.
No homework. No chores.
Eat. Nap. Call you up. Nap. Eat.
Three-day weekend spells RELAX.

Like a Feather Lifting

Like a feather lifts, floating on a breeze,
a pillow rolled behind my neck just right,
window cracked, a rustling of trees,
I spread my wings to dream of you tonight.
A barely moon set in a starless sky
where we can drift together, then apart.
Imagining the dance, I close my eyes
and tuck beneath your shoulder, ear to heart.
Although I know you're really blocks away,
inhaling, I can smell you next to me.
I dream about your smile, then press Replay,
what was, what is, and what is yet to be.
Our story takes so long to comprehend;
I fall asleep before I reach the end.

Celebrating Sleeplessness

Every ten minutes another message
arrives under my pillow and I respond
until they stop and I'm left on my bed
in the dark, flat on my back staring up
at the thought of you passing above
like a warm fog. My blood becomes
liquid electricity. My heartbeat
increases to feed the machine of me.

Does Superman sleep? Does gravity?
The turning world? A river? Me?

I finally reach over to turn on the light
and the room explodes with the brightness of you:
The clothes on the floor have washed
and folded themselves. From my window
I now have a view of the sea. The plant
on the sill that I slowly killed has sprung
back to life in the night. My homework
is done, every answer correct.

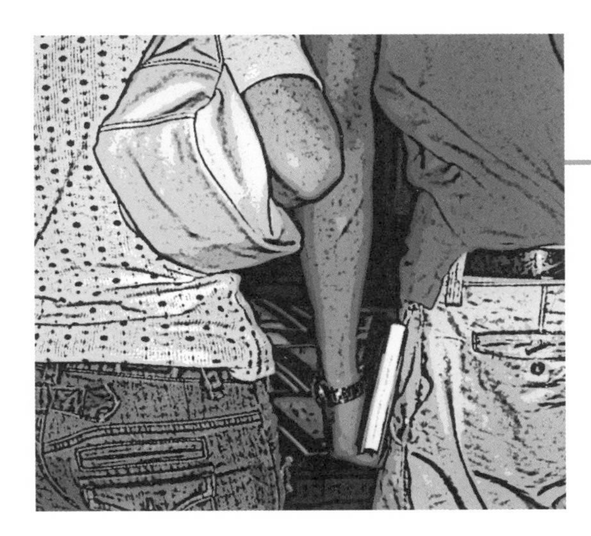

And though
it's only 4:00 a.m. I dress for school
and make a hearty breakfast:
I sprinkle you on my eggs.
I spread you on my toast.
I pour you into my juice glass.
Every bite seasoned by the thought of you.

Ninety minutes early, I leave for the bus.
The racetrack is quiet, all horses but me
asleep in their sunless stalls. Yet there I stand:
straining at the gate, waiting for your face
to sound the bell.

Cars

Him

Tricked out to the max.
Rims. Spoilers. Tint glass. Neon.
Thumpin' stereo.
Outside I'm the King of Bling.
Inside I'm Mom's old Volvo.

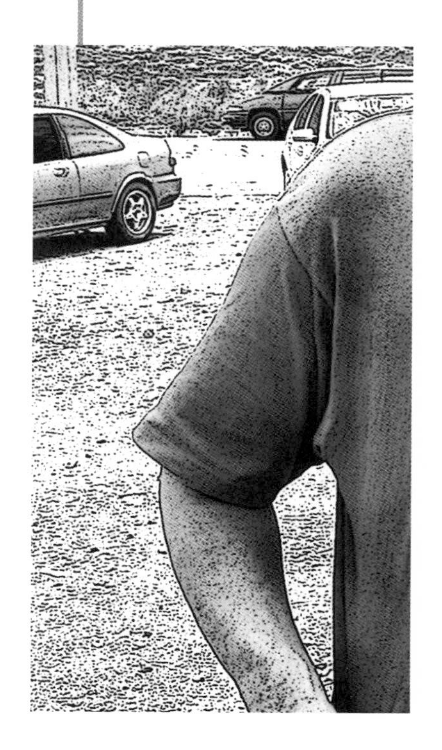

Her

I want my own keys
to independence. Four wheels,
heated leather seats,
trippin' in a 4x4.
Please. Just not Mom's minivan.

Fun

Her
Fun is a giggle,
pink lipstick, blue nail polish,
whispering girlfriends,
a good cry at a movie
then laughing all the way home.

Him
Fun is a joyride,
a spitting competition,
telling raunchy jokes,
laughing till our stomachs ache,
knowing that we all belong.

Food

Him
Calories don't count.
Quantity is paramount.
Biggie Super-Size.
Rice cakes? Hummus? They don't fly.
Only Whopper satisfies.

Her
Counting calories.
Translating fries to fat grams.
Weighing every bite.
My wants wrestle with my needs.
The exception: Chocolate.

With You, I'm Traveling Through This Strange Land

With you, I'm traveling through this strange land,
its population limited to two.
Here, thoughts pass wordlessly from hand to hand,
not understood except by me and you.
Beyond your face, the world's become a blur.
Our eyes are fused; the air's electrified.
What used to be a question now is sure.
Accepted, I've found comfort by your side.
It seems we've been together all along,
drawn here as if we knew the route by heart.
With you, I feel I finally belong.
Like magnets, we cannot be pulled apart.
I hope this magic journey never ends.
Except (big sigh) I kinda miss my friends.

Phone Call

Her

No, no. I can't go.
You-know-who is stopping by.
I'm supposed to wait.
Who knows? I can tell you this:
we're not headed to the mall.

Him

Yo, Damon. What up?
You got tickets? 'Course I'll go!
No way would I miss—
Oh. No. Wait. I've got a . . . thing.
That's cool. Y'all go . . . without me.

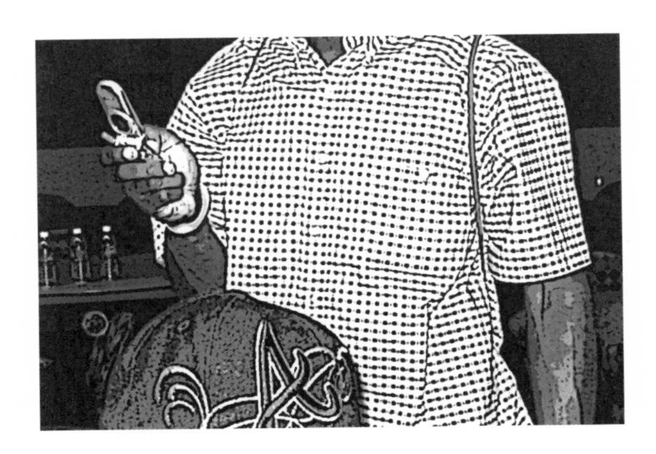

I Hope This Magic Journey Never Ends

I hope this magic journey never ends.
It makes me glad to see you every day,
Except (big sigh) I kinda miss my friends.

The road that lies before us twists and bends.
Intoxicated by the swing and sway,
I hope this magic journey never ends.

With every hour we share the road extends.
I rarely give a thought to yesterday,
Except (big sigh) I kinda miss my friends.

I do my best to try and make amends.
They call me "whipped," and yet what can I say?
I hope this magic journey never ends.

But still somehow uncertainty descends:
My conscience tells me not to swerve or stray,
Except (big sigh) I kinda miss my friends.

Now up ahead our easy pathway ends.
It splits in two. We'll have to choose a way.
I hope this magic journey never ends,
Except (big sigh) I kinda miss my friends.

Pleasing

Him

I try to please friends.
I try to please Mom and Dad.
Teachers, coaches, you.
I try to please everyone.
And lose myself in trying.

Her

Am I good enough?
I have no time. Let me help.
Is my laugh too loud?
You'll hate me if I say no.
When life's an act, who am I?

Friends

Him

If she is "just friends,"
then listen to what she says.
If she's your "*girl*friend,"
then listen to what she means.
. . . Or was it the other way?

Her

Talking openly.
Throwing popcorn at your head.
Teasing out a laugh.
So free. Like we were in fifth.
Could we find that place again?

She Only Wants to Talk to Me

She only wants to talk to me.
She never wants to touch.
She says,
Tell me why you love me and how much.
But when I try to *show* her,
she pushes me away.
And so I stand with empty hands and nothing right to say.

She says,
Tell me that you care for me.
That's what I'm trying to do!
She says,
We need to talk, or our relationship is through.

And so we slowly start to talk.
We talk of that. We talk of this.
Then once we're really talking,
all she wants to do is kiss!
Will someone out there tell me:

is there something that I missed?

I Absolutely LOVE You

I absolutely LOVE that Pistons shirt.
But don't you think one day a week's enough?
Relationships are fun, but also work.
I *have* to tease when you are acting tough.
I LOVE your friends, but Damon's on my nerves.
I LOVE your hair, but don't you need a trim?
I saw you checking out my girlfriend's curves.
You want to tell me where the heck you've been?
I try to squeeze my world inside of yours
and watch you watching football on TV,
so totally content, my heart just purrs.
Please turn that off and spend some time with me.
I LOVE we're pure perfection—it's all good!
I know you'll learn to call me like you should.

I Thought That Things Were Really Going Great

You knew, from jump, that I'm no fashion plate.
Now suddenly you're calling me a slob?
I thought that things were really going great.
You act like I'm applying for a job.
You want a full report when I'm not home.
The slightest misstep triggers your alarm.
While I admit my eyes do sometimes roam,
I look but I don't touch, so what's the harm?
If I appear defensive it's because
my *me* has been devoured by our *we*.
I thought that you were into who I was,
not into who you wanted me to be.
I thought we were a grand-slam hit home run,
but now I think we're going, going . . . done.

The Truth Revealed Between the Lines

I try to make us fit between the lines.
I try to make some sense of what I ***FEEL***.
I've tried to write it down a hundred times.
Our rhyme and rhythm's right, but are ***WE*** real?
I try to make us fit between the lines
and still stay true to who I want to be.
Is this verse yours to save or is it mine?
ARE you the one who's changed, or is it me?
We're ***MAKING*** an illusion that conceals
the easy lunchtime friends we used to be.
This sonnet's form is perfect yet reveals
A free-verse frenzy ***DEEP*** inside of me.
Make no ***MISTAKE***—I think you're really great.
It isn't you; it's *us* I sometimes hate.

You Want Chocolate Chip Cookies with That Order?

So let me get this straight:
it isn't *me*, it's
us you hate?
I should sweetly stand and wait
while you
bike, hike,
score, snore,
dunk, plunk,
drive, dive,
drum, strum,
and skate
and never question why you're late?
I don't remember making a proposal.
You think I was born to be at your disposal?

Warning!

At first we were just amorous.
Now suddenly we're serious?
She said "I love you." What's the rush?
I'm barely passing calculus!

The Flat Black in Your Eyes

The flat black in your eyes
no longer reflects
the laughter, the closeness
of us.
          Is it me?
Home? School? The bus?
Is it because of the game?
Does this darkening storm
have shape or a name?
          Is it me?
I listen.
I care.
You pretend I'm not there.
Okay.
Let's just sit.
Aren't we a pair?
Aren't we?
Or is it
          just me?

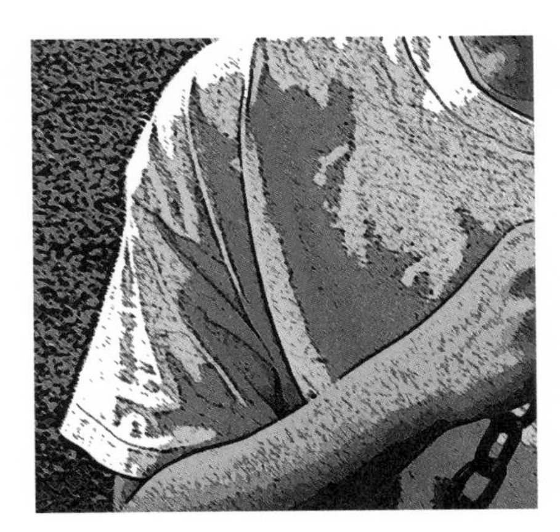

Alone

Him
Alone is a lake,
reflecting the aching moon,
searching the surface
for another of its kind,
finding nothing but false light.

Her
This no-makeup place,
no need to speak, smile, or comb.
Quiet thoughts whisper.
I cup my ear and lean in.
Listen! The sound of Alone.

Stressed

Him

Assignments, exams,
essays, practice, deadlines, grades,
friends, clubs, part-time job,
standardized achievement tests.
Yes, you might say that I'm stressed.

Her

Stress pulls my fingers.
Anxious, obsessed, I'm pacing
over the same ground,
dragging fear and guilt. Lost, late,
worried I'll never get there.

Angry

Him

I am *not* angry.
I am sad. I'm embarrassed.
I am frustrated.
Helpless. Humiliated.
Anger is only the mask.

Her

Sometimes I will lie
and say it doesn't matter
when, of course, it does.
Lies set fire to my insides.
Am I mad at you or me?

Depressed

Her

Depression is not
a sour look on my face.
Looks are a symptom
that my heart is deflated.
Trust and hope have gone missing.

Him

Depression is not
my voice becoming silent.
My silence is a symptom
of the sour look on your face.
Trust? Hope? Missing all along.

The Argument (for two voices)

Him	**Her**
You loved me like a cat loves a mouse.	
	I loved you like a mouse loves a trap.
I loved you like a mousetrap loves cheese.	
	I loved you like a hound dog loves fleas.
I loved you like a princess loves peas.	
	What?
I loved you.	
	I loved you.
I loved you.	I loved you.
You loved me like a foot loves a football.	
	I loved you like feet love to trip.
Like planes love to crash.	
	Like dry grass loves a match.
KABOOM!	*KABOOM!*

I loved you.	
	I loved you.
I loved you.	I loved you.
I loved you	
like a bomb loves a boom.	
	You loved me
	like a pin loves a balloon.
You loved me like worms love	
a tomb.	
	You made me fume!
	I loved you
	like bees love to sting.
I loved you	
when the phone didn't ring.	
	Hello! You made me stomp,
	kick, and curse.
So I wrote you this verse	So I wrote you this verse
because although our bad love	
nearly killed me	nearly killed me
without it,	
	no doubt about it,
I feel even worse.	I feel even worse.

Rejection

Him
Rejection hurts most
when you've opened up your heart
and let down your guard.
A flash-flood fist. A drop-dead
sucker punch to love-struck gut.

Her
A flutter of wings.
You ignore my outstretched hand.
My heart, a closed fist,
pounds at the wall of my chest.
What's wrong with me? No answer.

Feeling the Vibes

Broken nails,
fingertips raw and torn,
          burning
from wiping aside a stream of tears,
to scratching and clawing,
          pounding,
from trying to move this boulder.
One final kick only completes
the circuit of pain, head to foot.
          Then
ominous movie music swells,
foreshadowing danger.
A tremble of violins announces
          the approach.
Over the ridge a battalion
gathers on horseback
          clattering sabers.
I feel the vibrations of
thundering hooves and
crouch low,
knees to chest.
          They're coming . . .
regrets.

Apology

I held your landscape
To the light
And smudged my chest
With sunset,
A red orange swash across my heart.

I gripped your ocean
All too tight,
Effaced small crests
With groping,
A Moses making cat's-paws part.

I untidied your beach
With kicking digits,
Gawky thumbs,
Squawking birds;
My fingerprints basked on the strand.

Now finished and framed,
Old jealousies fidget:
An ocean undone,
A sunset blurred,
A ghost of my grasp in the sand.

Before You Knocked

Before you knocked, I was an empty room,
stripped of all anticipation.
Lonely me locked in a lifeless tomb.

My head was lost in clouds of hazy doom,
void of comfort, fire, and stimulation.
Before you knocked, I was an empty room.

Who could penetrate such hopeless gloom?
Could rescue me with love's illumination?
Lonely me locked in a lifeless tomb.

R.I.P. till you appeared—*kaboom*—
and saved me from my boring isolation.
Before you knocked, I was an empty room.

I heard your voice like a familiar tune,
calling me out of my desolation.
Lonely me locked in a lifeless tomb.

My swollen heart took off, a lost balloon,
though sometimes you caused major aggravation.
Before you knocked, I was an empty room.
Lonely me locked in a lifeless tomb.

Worth Repeating

Of love and verse the wise-at-heart declare
there is no novel note left to be sung,
that ancient love-struck poets filled the air
till no new word was left for future tongues.
Affection given, taken, lost, and found
by knights-at-arms on horseback, hearts afire
for damsels heaving sighs and woes: each sound
and circumstance transcribed for each desire.
But, though our lovelorn lines are nothing new,
recycled all through history, the fact
is romance never dies. So I loved you,
and for a happy while you loved me back.
No matter if these lines are overtold,
love's luster keeps them glistening like gold.

A Note from the Authors

Sara claims that this book was *her* idea. Allan insists it was *his* idea. Although we don't always agree and we live hundreds of miles apart, we've been friends a long time. No matter whose idea it was, writing a book together seemed like a fun way to stay in touch.

We e-mailed poems back and forth for nearly two years, and as our poetic conversation progressed we saw two distinct characters emerge from the words: a teenage guy and girl who are *just* friends at first, then *more* than friends, and finally just friends again. We simply stepped out of the way and let these two imaginary young people run the show.

Sara wrote the "her" poems. Allan wrote the "him" poems. We wrote sonnets. We wrote villanelles. Sara even contributed an uncommon form from Vietnam called a *luc bat*. Sometimes free verse seemed best for the job.

Throughout this book our two characters engage in what we have dubbed "tanka talk," a series of short poems about many topics. These poems represent the small talk between our couple as they get to know each other. Sara says the tanka talk was *her* idea. Allan claims it was *his*.

We know that Sara's poems don't represent the opinions of every young woman, just as Allan's poems don't speak for every young man. Still, we hope that this poetic conversation will help all "he's" and "she's" to celebrate their similarities while respecting their differences.

—Sara Holbrook and Allan Wolf

About the Poetic Forms

A football team runs set plays. A dancer moves to choreography. A skater glides through a program of spins and jumps. And a poet writes in forms. The following is a list of the poetic forms we used in *More Than Friends*. The definitions will make more sense if you check out the examples found in the book (see the page numbers listed with each entry below). This information is just a start. If you are a form fanatic, however, more detailed explanations are easy to find. And by the way, these forms are unisex, made for he-poets and she-poets alike. So take out your pen and try one on for size. —*S.H. and A.W.*

The Basics

Couplet

A pair of lines
that typically rhyme.

These days, rhymed couplets are popular in hip-hop and rap.

Tercet

Stanzas in three lines.
The verses may stand alone
like haiku (bless you!).

Some tercets combine
(see *villanelle* and *terza rima*)
in leaping, looping rhyme.

Quatrain

Mary had a little quatrain, (*a*)
poetic lines of four. (*b*)
She shared it with her poet friends (*c*)
who all cried out for more! (*b*)

Many popular song lyrics are written in quatrains, usually rhyming *a-b-c-b* or *a-b-a-b*. The quatrain *Warning!*, on page 49, rhymes *a-a-a-a*.

Refrain

The proper way to use refrain?
Say it once and then again.
Sometimes a poet repeats an expression.
Say it once and then again
in order to make a lasting impression.
Say it once and then again.
Say it once and then again.

The Forms

Free Verse (pages 10, 12, 14, 16, 24, 27, 36, 44, 48, 50, 57, 58)

Free-verse poetry (sometimes called open form) does not follow any strict rule of meter or rhyme. The poet determines the meter, line breaks, and rhyme on a poem-by-poem basis.

Luc Bat (page 13)

This Vietnamese form (pronounced LUK-BAHT, meaning "six eight"), alternates odd-number lines of six syllables and even-number lines of eight syllables. The sixth (the last) syllable of each odd-number line rhymes with the sixth syllable of the following even-number line. The eighth (the last) syllable of each even-number line rhymes with the sixth syllable of the following odd-number line. Oh, and the poem's last line must rhyme with the first! You really need to look at an example to get it. By the way, in the poem on page 13, we've thrown in an extra six-syllable line at the end.

Poem for Two Voices (page 54)

As its name implies, a two-voice poem is written to be read by two readers at once in alternating, overlapping, or unison lines. For more great examples, check out *Joyful Noise: Poems for Two Voices* by Paul Fleischman, the father of the multivoice poem.

Sonnet (pages 11, 18, 19, 31, 32, 35, 40, 45, 46, 47, 60)

Tap your toe, five beats to every line—two syllables per beat. Three quatrains and a couplet—fourteen lines that intertwine with alternating rhyme: *a-b-a-b, c-d-c-d, e-f-e-f, g-g*. The sonnet form used in this book is called Elizabethan (or Shakespearean). The Italian (or Petrarchan) sonnet form is a bit different. Whichever type you choose, the sonnet is as old as love itself—too sweet to be abandoned on the shelf.

Tanka (pages 12, 17, 20, 21, 26, 30, 33, 34, 38, 39, 41, 43, 51, 52, 53, 56)

Tanka is a five-line Japanese form that looks like a haiku with two extra lines attached. (A haiku has three lines, with five syllables in the first line, seven in the second, and five in the third [5-7-5].) The line-by-line syllable count of the tanka's English version goes like this: 5-7-5-7-7. Sort of like a haiku on steroids.

Terza Rima (page 22)

This Italian form finds balance in looping tercets linked by middle lines whose rhymes jump to the next stanza, like this: *a-b-a, b-c-b, c-d-c, d-e-d*. Place the rhyming lines in threes just right, you can loop-the-loop as long as you like. "Acquainted with the Night" by Robert Frost is one popular example of terza rima.

Villanelle (pages 29, 42, 59)

We have the French to thank for this rhythmical gem, which packs five tercets and one quatrain into a single nineteen-line poem. Inside those lines are two (count 'em, two) different refrains. The pattern goes like this: *refrain #1-b-refrain #2*, *a-b-refrain #1*, *a-b-refrain #2*, *a-b-refrain #1*, *a-b-refrain #2*, and finally the quatrain: *a-b-refrain #1-refrain #2*. The refrains both end with the *a* rhyme. The repetition resulting from the two rhyming refrains makes this poetic form pulse like a heart. To avoid injury, don't try this alone! Use another villanelle as a model when you start to create your own. Check out the villanelles in this collection, or refer to Dylan Thomas's famous example, "Do Not Go Gentle into That Good Night."